MIRRAN THOUGHT

MIRRAN THOUGHT

Spitzwiesenstr. 50
90765 Fürth
Germany

www.dwmirran.de
www.empty.de
empty@empty.de

READ TWENTY (MT-619)

Print and Publication by

BOD - Books on Demand
In de Tarpen 42
D-22848 Norderstedt
www.bod.de
info@bod.de

First printing 2019

MIRRAN THOUGHT is the publishing arm of
Mirran Threat, a company devoted to releasing the
music and writings of the various members of Doc
Wör Mirran. Mirran Thought and Mirran Threat are
both divisions of MT Undertainment.

HUMAN
BEING
HORNY

Western Haiku, Volume 9

Joseph B. Raimond

These pieces were written in Fürth, Germany between 2012 to 2015.

As always, in loving memory of Frank Abendroth and Tom Murphy.

Dedicated to Holger Czukay

For my beautiful Conny

Cover art "Human Being Horny"by Joseph B. Raimond, oil on canvas and wood, 2010.

This is DWM release Nr. 166

Fürth

A soft summer rain
Ruining my dry laundry
But I'm not mad

Has routine taken root?
Like all the weeds I battle
In my perpetual garden war

Give me a sign of life
Give me a sign of your love
My most powerful battle weapon

Butterfly, landing on a flower
Do you share my sorrows?
Do you understand my problems?

A poet sitting in the sun
Risking a sunburn
For a bit of inspiration

It just doesn't matter
It just doesn't matter!
In the end, it just doesn't matter

Never really woke up
From my afternoon nap
Still dreamin' of you

It is not the quantity
But the quality of your curves
And your love

A battle of the titans
As huge trees reach to the sky
Fighting for every ray of light

A soft summer midnight rain
Slowly filling my water tank
Tomorrow my plants will be happy

What should I call her?
This fat cat
Wanting milk at my door

The American dream: mobility
A family living in their car
The middle class drives away

Sometimes, throw a blind eye
To the horror of modern life
And watch a wonderful world

The sweltering heat beats
My head into rhythm
Drops of sweat, dripping

Saturday night, party night
Time for wine, women and song
Let's go!

She is worth every effort
To become that better person
You've been planning for so long

You have given me that hope
That was taken from me
Which I paid for in blood

Lovely little love letters
Sent back and forth
Save this mundane, working day

My head in your lap
As you stroke my hair
I think I'm in love

Black clouds, dark gloom
Smelling the promise of rain
My garden is thirsty

The sun beating down
Roasting my scalp
As I dream of snow

On the steps of Tiflis
We began our love, destined
For more than just a nice memory?

As the desert, grasping
For its few drops of water, saving
You suck me dry, tired and content

Sit back and enjoy, like a butterfly
Drinking at his flower, content
I will taste of your nectar

In this nightly, midnight gloom
Love, happiness, sun and warmth
Never existed, nor ever will

Tiptoe around that "L" word
Ssshhhh! Don't even whisper it
Once heard, you can never go back

I keep trying to fight it, deny it
But in the end I must give in, admit
That you do make me feel happy

A lazy Saturday afternoon
Sleep, read, booze, jerk off
And it is over far too soon

Laid back, this Sunday afternoon
Listening to old Badfinger albums
While repainting the bedroom

No! I won't accept summer is over
Millions, trillions of pretty colored
Leaves, will not convince me

Tell me, just how long do you plan
On haunting my mind, inspiring
Me to write hateful poetry

Just what could you teach me
Beautiful Dr. Lover
Eagerly, your student

Fizz, a bit of suds erupting
Cold beer dew
Creates rings on the wood table

Can age bring even beauty
Looking through the pretty green
Of your eyes, yes

Green eyed dreams of, love
Cradling my spirit
Through a lens of a cheap camera

Drudging through our daily routine
Kills what little passion might
Be left in our tired old bones

He's a life of his own it seems
Pulling me every which way
His quick thrills can ruin my life

Me and you, you and me
The only social network
I will ever need

Death!
To the first snow of winter
As the flakes melt on green leaves

Our secrets exposed, admitted
We laughed into the night
And made love into the morning

My castle, my world
I am its heart, soul
It is my body

Useless! Useless!
This year's holiday
Falling on a Sunday

The coffee's gone, news were on
Read to the end of the chapter
Time to get up and get to work

Another day, another love
Revolving door, take a number
But the heart is gaining numb

Don't judge me
For the sins of my father
Judge me for my own

Like hope we meet, rays of sun
When tears of past gloom nourish
Our seeds to reach the heavens

Take this moment
Live with it now, for who
Knows what tomorrow will bring?

On this wooden bench
I finally made that call
And cheated in my heart

A collection of….what?
Who cares, what it is!
As long as it is collectable

I've been learning the trade
Learning the ropes, to set sail
With you as my destination

It is raining, god is pissing
And we are all so thankful
Life is so fucking stupid

The Beatles, Star Trek, creamy
Peanut butter
Define me as a person

How exciting
Exhilarating, liberating, inspiring
To feel hope again

Although it is only weeks
You feel like a lifetime
Ago

This house in stillness, quiet
I achieved that time stands still
Where I may be happy to die

Autumn air, cold and crisp
Stings my nose, ruffles my hair
Breaths down my neck, chilly

In anticipation of you
I cannot work, I cannot think
I can only dream

At the risk of looking like a fool
I send you these few words
Heartfelt and honest, with love

Little boy playing, singing
Oblivious to oblivion
So happy in ignorance

Thirty, forty, fifty
My life, von null auf hundert
I live faster than a sports car

Like any other dog
Throw me a treat
And I'll love you forever

A rush, the brain in extreme
A stress to get the words down
Quick, as the dusk takes control

So damn fuckin' cold today
My nose is filled with
What looks like lime sorbet

Don't let the friendly sun fool you
Its warm smile doesn't hide
The bitter frozen cold it shines

Let's get blistered
Raw to the meat, red to the bone
Gasping in ecstasy and love

Even after a half century
The oblivion of sleep
Still scares me

These loves, so fragile
Threaten to break in an instant
Drag my heart along for the ride

Learning the signs
Learning the language
Of rejection, like an expert

So much wasted love
Lying around, getting dusty
While everyone waits for Mr. right

In that other, ugly world
A war, murder, someone is raped
In my world, a gentle rain falls

Army, harmy
A group of young, eager men
Ready to do their duty

Do this, do that
Putter around the house
Try not to feel bad

Hurricane boy went off to school
While daddy cleaned house
And waited for the next storm

I'll go ahead and say it
What no one else has the guts
Bob Dylan sucks

Their brains was bad
And their flags flew black
All I did was thump along

So simple, yet timeless
You inspire me again and again
You are truly immortal

The smell of linseed
The smell of inspiration
The smell of art

Smashing against my window
A stupid fly wants out
I release him to a frozen death

My house ain't burning yet
So I'm here kickin' back
Drinkin' a brew and waitin'

Colourful and bold, this graffiti
A nameless artist and his emotions
Urban inspiration on a train

November anchored,
Then come the blues
Give me your cure

Together, we were the universe
But then you left me
Apart we are nothing

If that is your idea of love, then
No man on this planet
Deserves your love

Dating is like robbing a bank
Grab what you can
Then run as fast as possible

An empty feeder outside
Birds waiting in the trees
For me to finish my coffee

You call it a gift
I call it persistence
And I know I'm right

Blood portraits will
Bleed
All that guilt away

I close my eyes
Feel the sun shining on my face
Filling me with happiness

Getting drunk on beauty
Music, the soundtrack to my life
Colors, forms, dance for my eyes

Cold day, so made a warm fire
A spider was hiding in the wood
Pain, a log dropped on my foot

Yellow lady, bringer of bad news
Your pile of little plastic windows
Go, give them to my neighbors

"To be continued…"?!?
If you continue,
Then only in the rubbish bin

No matter how cold the day,
It can still give warmth
To the winter that is your heart

Go away, give back
Give me back the heart
That you stole from me

The soldier can kill you
But the army
Kills him from the inside

I might even welcome
A slow, sleepy death
Painless, like falling asleep

My problem is
I never lost my starry notions
Along the way

The breathtaking beauty of a
Woman, all shot to hell
By the cigarette between her lips

No longer, do I try to be
What I never was
I now accept my faults, my style

Time heals no wounds
Rather, it lets them fester and rot
Within longing and regret

Fuzzy fur, we just want to pet
Hide the long fangs
Of my canine killer

I love her, but she loves another
And yet he loves someone else too
We all love, but are not loved

Let me give you something
Today, based not on greed
But on inspiration, (if I can)

Okay, okay! I'll take a shower
But you see, I can clean my body
But never my mind

To get that ugly old man
To fuckin' quit staring at me
I had to smash the mirror

Evolution:
Charles Bronson, Charles Branson
Charles Manson

The problems of today:
Are like a terminal pain
You get used to over time

Get rid of the hairy butts
Bubble boobs and phony groans
Porn would be okay

Wipe that smile off your face
Stop pretending all is well, when
Death is always a problem

Now: the golden age
Of isolation and misinformation
Mass consumption and weight gain

A thumb-sized snowflake
Lands on my considerable nose
It never stood a chance!

A crystal clear, big blue sky
Frozen with tranquil frost
Ignores the chaos of the street

Home, not only my castle,
But my world, my universe
My history

Comfy warm on my couch
Falling asleep, the TV fading
The best time of the day

Asleep, you were always prettier
And I, more in love with you
Than when I awoke

Throat begins to scratch
Nose runs, muscles ache
Inspiration suffers

Midnight noises, bonking
Dripping, clunking and dropping
Keeping me awake

Not just generations keep us apart
But circumstances,
Whispering tongues and envy eyes

We rocked, then went home
Tired and hung-over
Without fame, fortune or groupies

Stop, stop trying to influence me
Stop trying to sell to me
And stop insulting me

Today's sound, so shallow
No message, and hollow
My heart listens in sorrow

We fight the cancers
That ravage our bodies, but
Ignore our diseased minds

Holiday spirits soar
As the business men drool
The dollar signs in their eyes

Is old and alone
Just another word
For the freedom I so yearn?

Frankie went to Hollywood
Fell on hard times, was homeless
Got gunned down in a gang war

You were given the lives
Of the tired and homeless, and
Wasted them on TV and fast food

My wallet might be empty
But my heart is now free
I've found the cost of freedom

My mood is dark, mind is heavy
For the colour blue
Was never warm nor happy

Fuck the diet, screw exercise
Time for sex, drugs & rock 'n roll
I need a vacation from myself

Sickness, death, fire & destruction
The potential for misery and pain
Enjoy this life while you can

Another day, turns another year
And I celebrate in ignorance
The coming calamity and sickness

I'm jealous of you
Because of all the people
That came to your funeral

Time is like our lives
A year is a generation
You are my summer sun

Blood might be thicker than water
But blood brings rivers of tears
And wastelands of torn hearts

Twelve o'clock midnight,
Nothing seems to have changed
Our units of time are irrelevant

A few large glasses
Of water a day
Keeps the kidney stones away

Enslaved by our biology
We spend our lives lonely, in want
Reflecting on a moment of bliss

You can track every step I take
Read every word I write
Still, you will never know me

You watch TV all day
That's OK, I waste my time
Trying to figure out who I am

As one of billions
It is hard not to question
Our unique identities

Don't fall in love with me
Don't even like me
Don't do that to yourself

Too many years married
To a wicked despot
Has turned me into a socialist

As the days grow longer
And my mind starts to wander
I long for spring

Do rock the boat
Cause trouble, raise a storm
Start a revolution

Another turn towards freedom
Without getting lost in the clutches
Of the routine of torture

Sorry for what I did
Hope you can forgive me someday
But I just had to experience it

Breakfast cereal, cold, delicious
But absolutely no sugar!
Fulfills its purpose

For every poem in this book
Are a dozen that didn't make it
And a good one that got away

A whiskey in one hand
A girlfriend in the other
Being an adult is so....

What is this world coming to
When people care more about
Reality shows than art

Casualties counted, prisoners taken
On the estrogen front
In the perpetual war of the sexes

With such a mesmerizing smile
Certainly you are the one chosen
To complete my life

Fluttering through the air
A beautiful autumn leaf
Splat! Against my windscreen

Your bitterness so devours you
That you can't escape the hate
That destroyed what you love

This world
Doesn't give a fuck
If I am here or not

A winter banana
Cold, brown and mushy
Disgusting, destined for the trash

What kind of world is this
When Zappa is taken from us
And we are left with Ted Nugent

Insert creativity
Into your daily routine
Become a lifetime artist

Another pretty face
Beckons love, sex perhaps
At the very least, hope

Peanut butter on my breath
Flannel shirt, circumcised
I'm a real American!

My lips hurt
Worn out from kissing you
What a wonderful pain!

Let's go for a ride
We will never forget
Together, hand in hand

Lazy day, with time to think
Time to dream of you
And time to let you inspire me

Dazed and confused,
But in such a nice way
Your face reflected in my eyes

Your eyes, your words
Bring forth such a hope
I will leave my heart in your hands

I can't shake this feeling
That all roads led to you
And I have finally come home

I will happily spend this day
Dreaming of you
Time well spent

I was not made for celibacy
I was not made for loneliness
I was made for you

This day to day routine
Mundane, dull, highlights so few
Brighten, when I think of you

Such an expensive orgasm
Paid for not in dollars and cents
But in frayed nerves and patience

Wieners and scissors
And all that matters,
Like refugees, coming home

After years of starvation
Your paintings are a feast
For these hungry eyes

When words can be so shallow
The real truth lies
In the depth of my gaze

Don't feel sad, don't feel lost
Don't be mad, don't be cross
Learn to love the asshole I can be

I love the smell of books
The smell of the paper, the ink
The smell of culture and wisdom

A lifetime of learning
A lifetime of wisdom, hard earned
So little time to use it

The last cold breeze
Disappears
Weaker than a whisper

The lazy morning mist
Defies the hectic stress
Scheduled for this workday

Trying to force inspiration
I sit in my comfy chair, still
While my brain runs in circles

My cherry tree in bloom
A teenager, wooden puberty
Its pollen orgy invades my nose

Right handed, two left feet
Left hung, well hung
Self portrait

Leaf against leaf, rustling
The forest is an orchestra
The music of summer

Dandelion, a warm breeze
You take to the wind
Future weeds in my garden

Blooming flowers, I think of you
Singing birds and I think of you
Sunshine in my face, I think of you

Mating dogs, I think of you
Bouncing boobies, I think of you
A perfect ass, I think of you

"Do as I say,
Don't do as I do"
Was your marriage slogan

I aimlessly wander
The dark halls of my mind
They all lead to nothing

Bloody gash, invades
Conquers, the male mind
Leads him to insanity, longing

An angry dog
Attacked his abstraction
The world's only true artist

She suffered from pussy cancer
The men did not give a damn
Nor notice the tears in her eyes

Believe that I don't love you
It'll make it easier for you
To ignore my broken heart

Sunlight opens a flower
As a smile to the world
Your love is my sunlight

When we're good, we're great
But when we're bad…
Rainbows aren't black nor white

Give me solitude, alone
In a dark and secluded room
Over a room full of social people

The frozen man pretends love
All in a day's work
To get laid

Not afraid to try to kick your ass
But a mean word from my father
And I am a blubbering child again

I'll follow you down
As far as you might go
Just to help bring you back up

I am fed up with fleeting
I want permanence, stability
I want to live forever

Day for silent day
Your silence screams
Indifference at me

A few words without meaning
Say just as little
As your continued silence

Your face changes
Your name changes
Your love is interchangeable

First I found reasons to love you
Then reasons to leave you
I'm good at finding reasons

Let the days grow longer
Let time go by faster
Time to forget you

Sure, you taught me to laugh
But you were even better
In getting me to cry

Loving, arguments, indifference,
Up and down, the tides of our love
More powerful than an ocean

Eight cups of coffee a day
And two cupped breasts,
My life is measured in cups

Like a beautiful woman
I lock my paintings away
From the ugly eyes of the world

Your sex aint worth this stress
Aint worth the single tear
Finding its way down my cheek

I am fed up with your knowledge
Better move, so close to being sick
You aint gonna like what I puke

The problem with the highs
Are the inevitable, blue lows
Too weak to stop the tides

But I am color conscious
The shade of my blue t-shirt
Matches my mood perfectly

Stop, listen to the rustling leaves
Briefly, let time stand still
Before it ravishes me with age

Just why should a bird love
The depths of a deep blue sea
When it can soar to the sun

Thanks for the silence
It gives me time think
To convince myself I left you

I don't know where I'm going
But
I know I'll get there

In death, still jealous of you
All the cool people at your funeral
Who probably won't be at mine

A dog walking by, happy
Happy to see me, greet me
Suddenly, best friends for life

I'm a child of the corn
Don't worry, not going to kill you
At least, not now

Time marches on, dragging me
Kicking and screaming
Along with it

Beautiful woman, just how
Will you knock me off my feet
As a disillusioned couch potato

A jet has crashed, hundreds killed
Out there, somewhere,
So many mourning

Another face, another game
More indifference in the end
More meaningless, useless wisdom

Until science
Can make us immortal,
I will paint

The only good poet
Is the drunk poet
So pass the scotch

They said she was very sick
We said our goodbyes
I knew I would never see her again

Although the sun is high
And the warmth is friendly
An autumn crisp is in the air

My miracle love, fulfilling me
With youthful hope
The promise of a life I never knew

The beautiful animal
The deer, eating from my hand
Covering my hand with deer drool

The birds still sing
The nettles still sting
On this last day of summer

What a love, to render
Me, into a mass of sentimental
Happiness so strange

Lazy mornings of coffee
And early, passionate love
Doomed by routine and distance

The sun, still warms the day
But a cruel, cold night
Announces a lonely autumn

Like sickness
I have no patience for death
For both slow my art down

Let the dog out
Or even, let our secret out
But don't let our fire go out

The pain, like the big bang
Started infinitely small
But turned into a universe

This small house
With all its little tiny rooms
Home to a universe of love

Why must there be anything?
Nothing is so pure
In nothing there is no sadness

The more keys on your keychain
The more the responsibility
The less happy you will be

Every evening
To hold you in my arms
Is to give this home a purpose

No one really cares
About your art
Or mine

The biggest losers drive
The biggest cars
Show off your ignorance

I am not the center of the art world
But I am the center of my world
At least that is honest

Your incredible beauty
Really only results from
Your ability to have my children

The only good sex
Is old people sex
But only when the lights are off

A few misplaced words
Our carefully built house of cards
Comes crashing in hatred down

World peace is naïve, I know
How about harmony in these four
Walls, something I can hope for?

A lifetime of helling around
Is there really a deep faith
Ready to save one so lost?

Flowing water
Don't freeze as easy
Baby!

I've got my house
I've got my love
To hell with the world

First warmth, the spring sun shines
On me and my four-legged friend
This day was a gift

These last of cold days, the greyest
With a hint of invitation
Accepted by the blossoms born

In my book of romance
Written over a lifetime
You are the last chapter

Dog piss on a street lamp
Graffiti tags on a subway train
Dumb animals possess

It can't be a coincidence
That both a kiss and death share
X

Useless! Useless!
An ex-wife moving in
To my house or my heart

I don't think I'm left wing
I'm certainly not right wing
I have a fear of flying

I gave you a home
You turned it into a hell
And you were the devil

Millions, billions, perhaps trillions
Consciousness stolen by death
The sibling of time

Perhaps the last song is over
And the paint has dried
But a storm of words has begun

I am the champion ghoster
Walk away without a thought
To the tears that mourn

Crashing on the waves
Of my midnight sanity
The return of that pain in my gut

Your right to free speech includes
Screaming for help
In the hospital parking lot

Everyone stares at us, the worms
They see, we are in love
And we glow, like fireflies

Wonder bras hide wonder weapons
That have that wondrous bounce
That let all men look stupid

The bass strings wobble
So deep, so true
Give my heart a skip

Pretending to be immune
To petty office politics
I go home and pretend to ignore

Feeling half a century old
I was startled to realize
That I already was

As I ease into old age
And the memories fade
That little boy dies a bit more

As a beautiful summer sun shines
Only clichés gather in the mind
Of the uninspired poet

Bringing it full circle
To a close
I will end psychedelia

Useless! Useless!
The daily news
When I'm busy trying to feel good

A warm, summer night
Thunder booms in the distance
So I can feel immortal

For our immortal ghosts
I built a temple
But nobody came to worship

Useless! Useless!
Any and all exertion
On this hot, humid day

Little fire fly, trying so hard
To light up this big dark night
You did light up my soul

Preposterously plump,
The big sugar mama slurped
The gallon of cola under her arm

A sunny warm day
Family and friends on the porch,
And I almost feel human

As the ghosts ripped and tore
They set my spirit free
To find its way back to me

Move over, get out of the way
You're crowding out my greatness
With all your meaningless art

Hey, I'm an artist!
Stop ignoring me
Stop insulting my arrogance

A cool summer whisper
Breeze across my face
Promises the coming winter

George W. Bush swimmin' in a
Lake of brain-eating bacteria
He aint got nuthin' to worry 'bout

As a year flew by, kisses did fly
So much we ate, enjoying our fate
U made me a man, & a haiku ham!

So we are only at the start
Where my love for you comes
Always from my heart

No art, no music
No inspiration,
No thing

The spirit wants to accompany me
But I am so afraid
To be home again in the void

Who cares what happens outside
Within these four walls
I am a superstar

Love this little painting
It is the only immortality
I will ever have

Inspiration has done its job
The paint is drying on the canvas
I can go to bed now

Seconds, minutes, hours, days pass
Weeks, months pass, years pass
How did I get so old?

Her long, golden hair
Like a soft waterfall
Tumbles towards her breasts

As my sun begins to set
My restless soul finds no rest
The darkness thrashing, it won't let

Turning into my dad
Who turned into his dad
Generations of grumpy old men

How frustrating, for a man
That one so dumb to the bone
Can be so painfully sexy

That cheese that so insults
My nose as the fridge door opens
Melts on my tongue, in ecstasy

Turn away from the evil mirror
To get that ugly old man
Out of my face

A bit movement, then splash
A little green frog
Has jumped into my pond

As the evening moves on
The heaviest objects in the world
Are my eyelids

Only my boney old ass
Leaves such an obvious mark
On the seats of this old train

The sweaty, fat man's stench
Is terrorizing my nose
I've branded him a terrorist

Frank left the party early
I'll join him soon enough, though
Eternity is very patient

I'll never be the fifth Beatle
At this point,
I'd settle for the 379th

You're the world's biggest loser
And I should know,
As you lost me

After our petty row
We each brood in strategic silence
All really is fair in love and war

You robbed my little boy
Of his innocence, his smile
Is that of premature wisdom

My restless mind
Hasn't the patience of pen and ink
When it comes to inspiration

The dead are the lucky
The unborn the lottery winners
We the living are the chumps

They say misery loves company
And I love being miserable
So, wanna come to my party?

Don't leave me just yet
Your absence would hurt me so
And my pain is all that matters

Maybe if I just run away
And leave everything behind
The bad news won't find me

Time, abomination of nature
Always with enough patience
To kill us, slowly and cruelly

Let the percentages flow
Knock out the torment, for
Unconscious, I can't dwell

Out of breath in this race of life
Don't have the stamina
To even see the finish line

Greedy cheer, phony carols
For a saddened, grey morbid world
Happy holidays for a mighty dollar

Raimond's law of human nature:
The more wheels under the man
The bigger the asshole